T0196197

My View Through Grace

Karen Taylor

Scripture taken from the New King James Version®. Copyright © 1982 by Thomas Nelson. Used by permission. All rights reserved.

Scriptures taken from the Holy Bible, New International Version®, NIV®. Copyright © 1973, 1978, 1984, 2011 by Biblica, Inc.™ Used by permission of Zondervan. All rights reserved worldwide. www.zondervan.com The "NIV" and "New International Version" are trademarks registered in the United States Patent and Trademark Office by Biblica, Inc.™

Archway Publishing books may be ordered through booksellers or by contacting:

Archway Publishing
1663 Liberty Drive
Bloomington, IN 47403
www.archwaypublishing.com
1 (888) 242-5904

ISBN: 978-1-4808-6081-0 (sc)
ISBN: 978-1-4808-6083-4 (hc)
ISBN: 978-1-4808-6082-7 (e)

Library of Congress Control Number: 2018903440

Print information available on the last page.

Archway Publishing rev. date: 3/16/2018

Dedication

This book is dedicated to the many people over the years who have inspired me and kept me on my spiritual journey. To Dr. David Charlton, senior minister of First Christian Church, Shelbyville, Kentucky, thank you. Without your encouragement years ago, I would not have had the confidence to write this book. To my wonderful friends who have been trying to get me to write a book for years, thanks for the push. And finally, to my family, whose love and support have always been my rock, I love you all, especially, my soulmate and love of my life, Kenneth. His belief in me has never wavered, no matter how far I chased my crazy dreams.

Preface

As long as I can remember, I have wanted to be a writer and have dreamed of publishing a book. Dabbling a bit here and there, I have written articles for church newsletters, written some poetry, and even blogged for a few years. Blogging is where the writing bug really bit hard. My blog, titled *My View through Kat Eyes,* was my first real attempt at serious writing; I had to come up with my own topics and actually write something. I wrote about topics ranging from A to Z. The best part of it all was the wonderful writers I met from all over the world whose blogs inspired me to want to write even more. Problem was, I just couldn't decide what I wanted to write a book about. I had all these ideas running through my head, but I couldn't decide which one to write. That is, until we moved to western Kentucky and I took up my second secret desire, photography. Once I started getting a few pictures I thought were worth sharing, the plan started coming together in my head.

One of my favorite book genres has always been devotionals with beautiful scenic pictures that put me in a serene mood and let the devotionals really sink in. That's what I wanted to create. So that is how *My View through Grace* came about.

This book is for all of you who, like me, are still growing in your spiritual journey and sometimes struggle when times get tough. My prayer is that through my words and photographs, you may find a little peace and serenity along the way. May God bless you as you read these words.

A New Start

A new year, a new beginning. Time for renewal of the spirit. Each new year God gives me a clean slate to write my own story. What an amazing gift! How I use that gift is what defines me as an individual.

I don't make resolutions. Instead, I reflect on the blessings and trials of the previous year. Where am I in my spiritual journey? What changes do I need to make moving forward? Am I using my God-given talents in the way He intended? Am I doing enough to help those around me? Does my life reflect the love of Jesus Christ?

Unfortunately, the answers to these questions are all too often not the ones I seek. But one thing that continually remains constant is how deeply grateful I am for God's unconditional love and grace. His blessings flow abundantly, even though I fall short. And fortunately, each new year is another chance for me to get it right.

Start the New Year Right

Each New Year's Day we're given
a chance to start anew.
To think about what should have been
and mend a fence or two.
We think about the future and
try to find our best solutions.
And vow that this will be the year
we'll keep our resolutions.
There is a simple answer
to help you start out right.
Just give control to God above;
He'll guide you with His light.

Therefore, if anyone *is* in Christ, *he is* a new creation;
old things have passed away; behold, all things have become new.
2 Corinthians 5:17 NKJV

It brings me great comfort to know that not just at the beginning of the year but each and every day, God offers me a fresh start. I love the fact that even when I slip into old ways, He welcomes me with open arms. Forgiveness is a powerful and freeing vessel that guides me to new life in Him.

My faith doesn't assure me a pain-free life. Daily trials and hardships are always going to be a part of living. The one guarantee I do have is that I never have to face them alone. My belief in God provides the strength, the foundation, and the resource that allow me to deal with each situation as it comes.

Have I not commanded you? Be strong and of good courage; do not be afraid,
nor be dismayed, for the Lord your God *is* with you wherever you go.

Joshua 1:9 NKJV

A Miracle Child

A miracle child, sent from above,
Filled with spirit and contagious love.
A message from God, a light of hope,
Scott's life a witness of immeasurable scope.

On that glorious, beautiful, rainy day,
Our tearful goodbyes we tried to say.
"Ain't that pitiful," he surely said
As he looked down on the tears we shed.

"Don't cry for me," would be his plea.
"For now with Jesus, at last I'm free
To sing and dance and run and play
Till at heaven's gate we'll meet someday."

I believe there are special angels among us, sent by God for a purpose. One such angel was a child named Scott. Scott was the darling of an entire county, loved by all. He was a miracle child doctors said would never live past age six. God had another plan. Scott was here to teach us the true meaning of unconditional love.

Scott never walked, drove a car, or played sports like other kids. Yet he never felt angry or deprived. He never met a stranger and loved everyone. Once he knew you, he never forgot you. He could recognize anyone just by the sound of his or her voice. Scott had no filters or prejudice. Much to the chagrin of his parents, he often repeated things better left not repeated in front of anyone. That only served to make him even more endearing. His laugh was contagious. One of his favorite sayings was, "Ain't that pitiful?" He loved to tell you to say it for him and then clap your hands.

Scott's favorite place to go was church. He loved singing hymns at the top of his lungs, and he especially loved the people. He loved his Lord, and he wasn't afraid to let everyone know it. No matter where he was. That kind of unhindered spirit is rare.

Scott lived to be forty-two. In those forty-two years, he touched the lives of more people and taught us more about loving and appreciating life than most so-called healthy people. Scott never once thought of himself as different or handicapped. He was the happiest person I ever met, and knowing him was a true blessing. He simply loved life and loved people. He taught me so much. God wouldn't entrust the care of such a special angel to just anyone. His family are great friends. They continue to be inspirations and blessings to those who know them.

Create in me a clean heart, O God,
And renew a steadfast spirit within me.
Psalm 51:10 NKJV

Knowing God's Love

You see it in his laughing eyes and in his quiet grace.

You see that something special, shining in his happy face.

You feel it in his gentle touch and hear his soulful glee.

This is no ordinary clown. What could the difference be?

You want to know this kind of joy!

He says it's from above.

If you only open up your heart, like the clown, you'll know God's love.

Before clowns became something to be afraid of, they were beloved symbols of childhood, evoking thoughts of parades, circuses, and happy times. Several years ago, I had an alter ego known as Blossom. My sister, Jane, and I, along with a few others, formed a Christian clown troupe called The SonShine Troupe. Through joy and laughter, we were able to present the gospel at churches, Bible schools, nursing homes, and anywhere else we were asked. It was one of the most rewarding experiences of my life.

If everything we do was done in love, how much nicer could we make the world around us! Every day we have a choice on how we are going to face the day. Make a conscious effort each morning to be the best version of yourself that you can. A simple smile can warm a cold heart and start a chain reaction that may reach farther than you will ever know.

A merry heart does good, *like* medicine,
But a broken spirit dries the bones.
Proverbs 17:22 NKJV

Kindness Could Change the World

The world would be a perfect place if everyone were kind.
If each could see another's need instead of being blind.

It doesn't take much effort to give someone a smile,
Or lend an ear or helping hand to cheer them for a while.

A random act of kindness might only take a minute,
But it could change a stranger's life if your heart and soul are in it.

Love must be sincere. Hate what is evil; cling to what is good. Be devoted to one another in brotherly love. Honor one another above yourselves. Never be lacking in zeal, but keep your spiritual fervor, serving the Lord. Be joyful in hope, patient in affliction, faithful in prayer. Share with God's people who are in need. Practice hospitality.

Romans 12:9–13 NIV

Love

A simple four-letter word that even the youngest among us understands. It is probably the most overused word in the English language. We casually throw the word around, referring to everything from our family to pizza. I'm not sure this is what God intended. Love should come from the heart. As the scripture says, it must be sincere. God loved us enough that He created us in His image and then sent His Son, Jesus Christ, to die on the cross for our sins. That, in itself, humbles me to my very core. It fills me with a love so intense it can't help but overflow. If He could love me that unconditionally, shouldn't I live my life loving others in return?

Though I speak with the tongues of men and of angels, but have not love, I have become sounding brass or a clanging cymbal. And though I have the gift of prophecy, and understand all mysteries and all knowledge, and though I have all faith, so that I could remove mountains, but have not love, I am nothing. And though I bestow all my goods to feed the poor, and though I give my body to be burned, but have not love, it profits me nothing.

Love suffers long and is kind; love does not envy; love does not parade itself, is not puffed up; does not behave rudely, does not seek its own, is not provoked, thinks no evil; does not rejoice in iniquity, but rejoices in the truth; bears all things, believes all things, hopes all things, endures all things.

Love never fails. But whether there are prophecies, they will fail; whether there are tongues, they will cease; whether there is knowledge, it will vanish away. For we know in part and we prophesy in part. But when that which is perfect has come, then that which is in part will be done away.

When I was a child, I spoke as a child, I understood as a child, I thought as a child; but when I became a man, I put away childish things. For now we see in a mirror, dimly, but then face to face. Now I know in part, but then I shall know just as I also am known.

And now abide faith, hope, love, these three; but the greatest of these is love.

1 Corinthians 13:1–13 NKJV

Blessed are the pure in heart,
For they shall see God.
Matthew 5:8 NKJV

The View from My Window

Out my kitchen window, the view that I can see
Is comforting and peaceful and beautiful to me.
Cows are in the pasture; the barn is on the hill.
Ducks are floating in the creek, looking for a meal.
The trees stand tall and barren; their leaves are on the ground.
The fields show signs of winter creeping in without a sound.
A tractor in the distance reassures all is right.
The warmth I feel comforts my soul and makes the world seem bright.
I love to look out on our farm as dusk begins to fall.
I see the glory of God's plan for farmers one and all.

And be kind to one another, tenderhearted, forgiving one
another, even as God in Christ forgave you.

Ephesians 4:32 NKJV

Kindness is a rare commodity these days but one that costs us nothing. Practicing kindness will not only benefit those on the receiving end but also change your whole attitude. The more you practice, the more being kind will become ingrained in your subconscious. Soon you will not only be a nicer person but also be a much happier person.

It's becoming increasingly common to get down on ourselves when we think we aren't the best, smartest, or most beautiful. God made you a unique and wonderful person just the way you are. True beauty comes from the heart. Anyone whose heart is kind and genuine will always be a success in God's eyes and, therefore, beautiful.

Therefore humble yourselves under the mighty hand of God, that He may exalt
you in due time, casting all your care upon Him, for He cares for you.

1 Peter 5:6–7 NKJV

I will meditate on the glorious splendor of Your majesty,
And on Your wondrous works.

Psalm 145:5 NKJV

It is hard for me to understand how anyone can look at the beauty of nature and not see the glory of God's creation. After all these years, I am still awed at the sight of a rainbow or a beautiful sunset. It fills my heart with tremendous joy to know that He created all of this for us.

Spread it Around

A kind word of encouragement, a hug or just a smile,
Can warm a heart and fill the soul with gladness for a while.

You can start right where you are; spread sunshine everywhere.
You'll feel a change come over you, like a kid without a care.

You'll find joy is contagious if passed around with love.
The world will be a better place, and God will smile above.

Trusting God

The year 2017 brought major life changes for my husband and me. After being a dairy farmer all his life, my husband finally retired, and we moved nearly three hundred miles from almost everything and everyone we had ever known. Not an easy decision at our age. The reason for this move was to be closer to our son, daughter-in-law, and two grandchildren. As we are getting older and have both dealt with numerous health issues, we knew we needed to be near them to make it easier on all of us. Even knowing that, it was still the most difficult decision we ever made. We wanted to be closer to our kids; that was easy. We love them more than life itself and have already missed out on so many years with them. But on the other hand, we left brothers, sisters, and friends behind whom we were close to all our lives. It was exciting and extremely scary all at the same time.

Left on our own, I'm not sure we could ever have made the final decision. It took many days and hours of prayer. God had a plan, and He knew what was best. We put our trust in Him, and He made it clear this was our new path. It has been an adjustment, but overall, things couldn't have worked out better. Our fear of making new friends and finding a new church home have all been alleviated. And the blessing of spending time with our children is beyond measure! This is where God meant for us to be.

Turning everything over to God in prayer is sometimes a hard thing to do. I really struggle with hanging on to control. When I don't give it up, that's when I make mistakes. Prayer is a personal conversation with God, a conversation that goes two ways. In order to hear His response, we must open our hearts and our minds and be receptive to His guidance. Sometimes that response may come like a bolt of lightning. Other times it may be as soft as a whisper. Either way, He is on our side.

There are different kinds of gifts, but the same Spirit. There are different kinds of service, but the same Lord. There are different kinds of working, but the same God works all of them in all men.

1 Corinthians 12:4–6 NIV

As each one has received a gift, minister it to one another, as good stewards of the manifold grace of God.

1 Peter 4:10 NKJV

Just as each of us has one body with many members, and these members do not all have the same function, so in Christ we who are many form one body, and each member belongs to all the others. We have different gifts according to the grace given us. If a man's gift is prophesying, let him use it in proportion to his faith. If it is serving, let him serve; if it is teaching, let him teach; if it is encouraging, let him encourage; if it is contributing to the needs of others, let him give generously; if it is leadership, let him govern diligently; if it is showing mercy, let him do it cheerfully.

Romans 12:4–8 NIV

The above verses are some of my most favorites. What a relief to know that God doesn't expect me to be just like everyone else. Each of us have unique God-given gifts or talents. All are equally important. Finding and using those talents is essential to being a loyal follower. God expects us to use our gifts, no matter how small. Your gift may be as simple as being a good listener, helping a lonely neighbor, or being a good organizer. Whatever it is, don't waste it. Find every opportunity to put it to good use.

Peace, Be Still

"Peace, be still," I'd heard it said;
The words kept running through my head.
But the words that took control of my mind
Were of fret, worry, and the anxious kind.
Anxiety grew till I'd reached the end;
I felt like I'd lost my last friend.
As I sat and looked in the mirror one day,
I suddenly lifted my hands to pray.
I prayed to God to lift my spirit,
Not even sure if He would hear it.
Then, "Peace, be still," I heard Him say,
"Just let me take control today."

He Lives in Me

Since He came into my life, a peace within me flows.
It warms my soul and fills me till I'm certain that it shows.

He gave His life to save me as well as every other.
But in return He only asks we love Him and one another.

I'll let my light shine for Him in every way I can,
By telling of the miracle when God became a man.

He gives His love so freely, and I can only try
To live for Him and share that love till I meet with Him on high.

Therefore, having been justified by faith, we have a peace with God through our Lord Jesus Christ, through whom also we have access by faith into this grace in which we stand, and rejoice in hope of the glory of God.

Romans 5:1–2 NKJV

Finding peace in today's chaotic world would be impossible if not for my faith. Prayer, Bible study, and fellowship give me a grounded foundation that helps me face whatever the world throws my way. Because of God's amazing grace, I am able to find peace and strength when all else is failing.

Therefore, whatever you want men to do to you, do also to them,
for this is the Law and the Prophets.
Matthew 7:5 NKJV

The Golden Rule

We've all heard it since we were kids: "Do unto others as you would have others do unto you." Unfortunately, many people would probably guess Mother Goose rather than the Bible if they were asked where it came from. But there it is in black and white, in chapter 7 of Matthew. Think how wonderful this world would be if everyone practiced this simple verse. We would live in a world with no wars, no hatred, no prejudice, and no crime or deception. Everyone would get along. Just imagine! Maybe we can't change the whole world, but we can make a difference. Change must come from within your own heart. Learn to practice the golden rule, and you might begin to see a difference one person at a time.

These things I have spoken to you that My joy may remain in you, and that your joy may be full. This is My commandment, that you love one another as I have loved you. Greater love has no one than this, than to lay down one's life for his friends.

John 15:11–13 NKJV

Beloved, let us love one another, for love is of God; and everyone who loves is born of God and knows God. He who does not love does not know God, for God is love. In this the love of God was manifested toward us, that God has sent His only begotten Son into the world, that we might live through Him. In this is love, not that we loved God, but that He loved us and sent His Son to be the propitiation for our sins. Beloved, if God so loved us, we also ought to love one another.

1 John 4:7–11 NKJV

A Special Gift

God knew we weren't suited to drift through life alone.
He knew we'd live in misery if left all on our own.
That's why He gave us friendship to fill our hearts with love;
To be our constant lifeline, like angels from above.

Friends share life's emotions, whether good or bad.
They laugh with you in good times and comfort you in sad.
True friends stand beside you when push may come to shove.
They are a special blessing, a gift from God above.

Joined by God

When hearts are joined by love alone,
The union may not last.
But when that love is bound by faith,
Soon many years have passed.
No matter what those years have brought,
You faced it side by side.
Commitment, faith, and love grew strong
When God your path did guide.
Now friends and family share your joy
As you celebrate your love.
And for the blessings He bestowed,
Give thanks to God above.

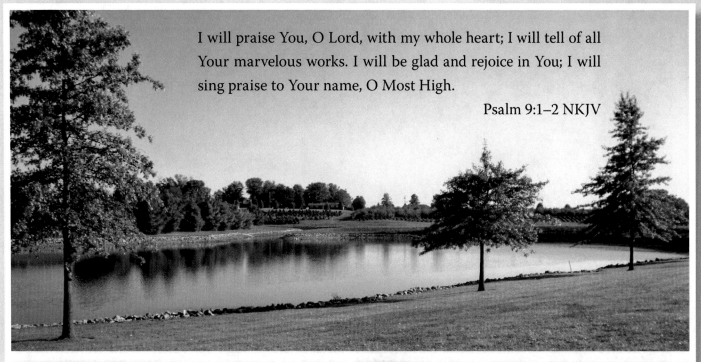

I will praise You, O Lord, with my whole heart; I will tell of all Your marvelous works. I will be glad and rejoice in You; I will sing praise to Your name, O Most High.

Psalm 9:1–2 NKJV

God's Glory

The beauty of a rainbow, sprawling through the sky.
The glory of the autumn leaves as their brilliant colors fly.

The joy of a newborn baby when you hold him in your arms.
The pride you feel as he grows up, and all the girls he charms.

If you should ever start to doubt the miracle of God's creation,
Just stop and look around you with renewed appreciation.

Take the time to ponder on God's great and awesome glory.
Don't miss the beauty of each day and tell His wondrous story.

Oh come, let us sing to the Lord! Let us shout joyfully to the Rock of our salvation. Let us come before His presence with thanksgiving; Let us shout joyfully to Him with psalms. For the Lord is the great God, And the great King above all gods.

Psalm 95:1–3 NKJV

Jesus answered him, "The first of all the commandments is: 'Hear, O Israel, the Lord our God, the Lord is one. And you shall love the Lord your God with all your heart, with all your soul, with all your mind, and with all your strength.' This is the first commandment. And the second, like it, is this: 'You shall love your neighbor as yourself.' There is no other commandment greater than these."

Mark 12:18 NKJV

My Special Place

When I'm in need of comfort, there's a place I always go.

When I'm feeling sad or lonely, it will lift my spirit so.

The people there are friendly; they love and care for me.

They welcome me with open arms; they fill my heart with glee.

But even when there's no one there, my soul can still find peace.

I think and pray in solitude until my worries cease.

This haven is no secret; there's lots of room for you.

The doors are always open, and the invitation too.

My church is such a special place; I find a solace there.

The power of God's presence assures me of His care.

Rejoice always, pray without ceasing, in everything give thanks; for this is the will of God in Christ Jesus for you.

1 Thessalonians 5:16 NKJV

Make a joyful shout to the Lord, all you lands! Serve the Lord with gladness; Come before His presence with singing. Know that the Lord, He *is* God; *It is* He *who* has made us, and not we ourselves; *We are* His people and the sheep of His pasture. Enter into His gates with thanksgiving, *And* into His courts with praise. Be thankful to Him, *and* bless His name. For the Lord *is* good; His mercy *is* everlasting, And His truth *endures* to all generations.

Psalm 100:1–5 NKJV

Families Are Like Puzzles

In his later years, my dad's favorite hobby was working jigsaw puzzles. It would be impossible to guess how many he completed. Some had only a few pieces, and others maybe a thousand. Some fell into place easily, taking only a short time to complete. Others took him months of diligent work to fit all the pieces together. In the end, he had a beautiful work of art.

I couldn't help but see the correlation between those puzzles and a family. Some families are made up of only a few individuals, while others may have many. Of those individuals, no two are alike. Some are straitlaced, like the border that provides the guidelines of the family. Others may be a little square, like the cornerstone that keeps the family grounded. Then, of course, you have the various shapes and sizes with their own personalities who keep things interesting, if not a little difficult at times.

Like a puzzle, a family requires all these components to make a complete unit. Families have a way of fitting together in spite of individual differences to form a unified circle of love, support, and harmony. That doesn't mean they always agree or that everything comes easily. But when the chips are down, family comes together. In the end, you have a beautiful work of art.

A Father's Love

A father's love may go unsaid,
    But it won't go unseen.
He's always there to hold your hand.
    Your rock on which to lean.
He builds in you an inner strength
    By setting an example.
No matter what demands life brings,
    His time for you is ample.
He's always there when times are tough
    To mend your busted toy;
Through homework, hopes, and broken dreams,
    He shares both pain and joy.
He's mentor, friend, and confidant.
    He teaches wrong from right.
He proves no matter what the cost,
    In life, love's worth the fight.
A father has a special role,
    Filled first by God above.
Through hard work, pain, and sacrifice,
    He fills our lives with love.

A Mother's Love

A mother's love is like no other,
    A force you can't explain.
No matter what the sacrifice,
    She never will complain.
Her love is everlasting.
    You never have to fear.
She'll share your joy, and feel your pain;
    She always will be near.
She'll pick you up whene'er you fall.
    She'll kiss the pain away.
She'll always lend a listening ear
    And know just what to say.
Her tender touch can soothe your soul;
    Her smile can warm your heart.
She shares life's special moments,
    Even when you're far apart.
There are few things in this world today
    On which you can depend.
But a mother's love is certain;
    It's a bond that knows no end.

Grandparents

I look to you when I need advice
For the wisdom of your years.
When worldly comforts won't suffice,
You always dry my tears.

You always know just what to say
To take away my worry.
You tell me tales of olden days,
When life wasn't such a hurry.

Love's a bond that can't be broken,
Nor measured where it starts.
But even when words go unspoken,
They're felt deep in our hearts.

Honor your father and your mother, that your days may be long upon the land which the Lord your God is giving you.

Exodus 20:12 NKJV

I believe honoring your parents extends to grandparents. Being a grandparent is the greatest gift in the world, next to being a parent. I never got to have the relationship with most of my grandparents that I would have liked to. Three of them died while I was a child. The one who lived long enough for me to really get to know him was Grandad Seacat. He was a character, and I loved him dearly. I was sorry my son never got to know him; he passed a few months before my son was born. My point is, life is short. We never know how long we have to form relationships with those we love. Never take that time for granted. Appreciate each day you are given. Take the time to love those around you. Really get to know your family. Love them unconditionally.

Lessons Taught

Do you know who's really watching when you think no one's around?

Do you realize the lessons taught, sometimes without a sound?

Children watch each step you take; they read you like a book.

They see behind the false façade we use when friends can look.

They see what's really in your heart; they learn by your example.

Are you sincerely kind and good? Is your love for others ample?

What values are you planting by a thoughtless act or deed?

Are they seeds of love and kindness, or prejudice and greed?

Remember you must "walk the walk" and not just preach the Word.

A child learns more by seeing than by anything they've heard.

I'm Thankful For ...

Thanksgiving is here,
    the turkey is done.
There are parades to watch,
    football games to be won.
Then finally, everyone's out of the house,
    I've time to myself to ponder
The many things I'm thankful for,
    so many my mind starts to wander.
I'm thankful for my Savior
    and how He's blessed my life.
He led me to the perfect man,
    Whose love made me a wife.
A son who made us very proud
    has a family of his own.
What joy they bring into our lives;
    How our circle of love has grown.
My list of special blessings
    is too numerous to name.
Not only on Thanksgiving Day
    but every day the same.

With all my heart, I give my thanks
    for blessings from above.
I praise my God, who guides my life,
    and saved me with His love.

And suddenly there was with the angel a multitude of the heavenly host praising God and saying: "Glory to God in the highest, And on earth peace, goodwill toward men!"

Luke 2:13–14 NKJV

Like the shepherds in the field that eventful night, I stand in amazement at the wonder and glory of the reason we celebrate Christmas. I am humbled by the fact that God loved me enough to send His only Son as atonement for my sins. I love the Christmas season, and I never let myself forget its true meaning. Love came down at Christmas, and it never left. How wonderful is that?

Not Just at Christmas

It's like a metamorphosis;
The change is very clear.
It's everywhere, in everyone,
And starts this time each year.
You see the transformation
On each face and in each heart.
You see the love and mercy,
Feel the kindred spirit start.
Peace, goodwill to all mankind
Is such a simple theme.
Its universal language
Was part of God's grand scheme.
The Christ child came at Christmas,
God's greatest gift of love,
To save the world from sin and loss,
And guide us from above.
God's love is constant, without fail.
We shouldn't need more reason
To love our fellowman all year,
Not just the Christmas season.

Oh, give thanks to the Lord, for *He is* good! For His mercy *endures* forever.

1 Chronicles 16:34 NKJV

Rejoice always, pray without ceasing,
in everything give thanks; for this is the
will of God in Christ Jesus for you.
1 Thessalonians 5:16–18 NKJV

The Reason for Christmas

Lights and decorations are hung upon the tree.

We sing our favorite carols in perfect harmony.

Familiar signs of Christmas are everywhere we look.

Just like a Dickens village come to life right from a book.

We shop and bake and decorate; we hurry to and fro.

We must have all the work done by Christmas Eve, you know.

But do you ever wonder as you tie the last bow tight,

Is this what Christmas really is; am I doing this all right?

God sent a child so long ago, and He should be the reason

To celebrate in humble praise; put Christ back in the season.

For God so loved the world that He gave His only begotten Son, that whoever believes in Him should not perish but have everlasting life.

John 3:16 NKJV

Printed in the United States
By Bookmasters